Grow Gracefully:

Journey To Wholeness

By Jennifer Clark

Copyright 2024 by Jennifer Clark

ISBN 978-1-304-77887-1

All rights reserved.

Table of Contents

1. Do You Want to Be Made Whole?
2. Say No
3. Heart Check
4. The Time Is Now
5. How Well Do You Know Yourself?
6. That's What Friends Are For
7. Half Empty or Half Full?
8. Red Light, Green Light
9. Likes, Comments, Follows
10. Lessons From the Mountains
11. Who's Calling?
12. Practice the Pause
13. Time to Switch!
14. Bounce Back
15. Nothing Hidden
16. Up Close and Personal
17. Don't Settle
18. You're Almost There
19. Get In Shape
20. Hello 40!

Chapter 1

Do You Want to Be Whole?

The Chinese philosopher Lao Tzu once said, "A journey of a thousand miles begins with a single step." Life is truly a journey as we have covered many miles along the way! Along the journey, we have encountered ups, downs, exciting times, challenging times, and confusing times. I don't know about you, but I have had my share of experiences of heartache, brokenness, and disappointments over my life. And 2020 alone... whew!!! What a year it was! Our world experienced a pandemic like none other when the coronavirus swept through and changed lives forever. Then, 2021 and 2022 came along and the pandemic was still around. Last year in 2023, we were still being impacted by the effects of the virus as life looked different in so many ways. Not only was a worldwide pandemic happening, but many of us experienced personal hardships at the same time. In 2020, three of my family members lost their lives. All our losses were on my Mom's side of the family. My Mom, aunt and grandfather all left us within the first six months of 2020. It was one of the hardest seasons of my life. In that same year, many other families also lost their loved ones from the virus and from other causes. My heart goes out to all the families because I can relate. Not only did I lose family members in 2020, but I also faced disappointments, shattered dreams, and dark and lonely moments that words cannot even begin to describe. But I can truly say (and I know I have others with me!) that God is the reason I'm still standing.

Even though 2020 was the toughest season of my life, it was also a season of growth and healing for me. A lot of lessons came out of that season and the seasons that followed, which I will share with you throughout this book. I am still healing and still growing as it is an ongoing process. We cannot avoid the storms of life, but we can choose how we respond to the storms that come. Instead of making New Year's resolutions in the past years, I have instead chosen a word to focus on. In the past, I have chosen words, such as hope, confidence, transformation, truth, and identity. When praying to God for what my word should be for the year 2021, He gave it to me on New Year's Eve morning 2020. My word was wholeness! To be whole means to be complete and not wounded or damaged. As I mentioned earlier, I have been wounded in many ways. 2020 showed me that healing is possible. Even though I have had new words since 2020, I am still working on being whole. I still need to be focused on being well in my mind, body, and soul. When one is off, it affects the others. My desire is to be whole in all areas of life. Therefore, I decided to say yes to the wholeness journey. I know I still have work to put in to become whole, but I am willing to do my part. I want to keep hoping, keep believing, keep expecting. Throughout this devotional, I will talk about how we can pursue and take steps to wholeness on our life journey. So, what do you say? Do you want to be made whole? Will you join me and say yes to the journey? If you are ready to say yes, then let's continue our journey to wholeness!

Chapter 2

Say No

"No." One word, yet it has so much power. By itself, "No" is a complete sentence. When someone says no, that means he or she is not accepting something, not agreeing with someone or something, or choosing not to do something. Saying no will cause different responses from different people. Some will be okay with it. Some will be confused by it at first, then let it go. Some will question your "no" and want you to explain why you answered the way you did. Others will even try to make you feel bad for answering the way you did. The truth of the matter is you do not owe anyone an explanation. A no is simply just that. It is an answer all by itself and should be respected. It is okay to say no. While we may not always like hearing the answer "no," we must accept it and still respect the person that gave us the answer. For some of us, we do not like saying no. It may be hard and uncomfortable to say, but it is something we need to do on our wholeness journey.

To become whole, there are some things and people we must let go. That requires us saying no to those things or people. I want to take it a step further and say we need to say no to certain social media accounts. Every page should not be followed and viewed. Every friend request should not be accepted. We need to say no to unhealthy lifestyles and relationships. We need to say no to things that bring us down and drain us. We need to say no to wrong and stretching ourselves too thin. You know how we can take on too many projects at one time and then our plates get too full!! We cannot pour into anyone else if we are empty! I am constantly reminding myself of this. I used to feel so guilty and thought it was bad to tell people no. Thank goodness for growth in that area! Now I know better and am quicker to say no. I am learning that saying no can be a good thing.

When we say no to certain things, it can change our whole outlook on life. It must be a daily practice. I'm not going to tell you that it will always be easy to say no, especially when you're used to saying yes all the time. It still gets hard for me at times. Asking God for wisdom about when to say no and what to say no to is crucial (James 1:5). Some things do need our yes, while other things need to be given a no. Comparison, complaining, backbiting, unforgiveness, bitterness and jealousy need a no. Low self-esteem, unhealthy relationships, mixed signals, inconsistency, worrying, overthinking, and overcommitment also need a no. None of those things will help us to become whole. They will weigh us down and keep us from moving forward. Start today by saying no to what is not good. Saying no will change your life and my life...for the better!

Chapter 3

Heart Check

How's your heart doing? Our physical heart has a huge job in keeping us alive! Our heart is constantly pumping blood through our body. Our heart works hard to make sure our blood flows as it should. We can keep our physical heart healthy by exercising, eating healthy foods, and reducing stress. When healthy choices are made, we lower the risk for heart disease. If we work that hard to take care of our physical heart, why not work that much harder to take care of our spiritual heart?! The word heart is mentioned many times in Scripture. In Mark 12:30, it talks about how we should love God with our all. It first mentions we should love God with all our heart. All means whole and not lacking anything. It means to be fully committed and giving it everything we have. It is more than saying we love God in words. It must be shown in our actions as well. Jesus talked about the religious leaders in Matthew 15:8 and said how they honor Him with their words, but their heart was far from Him. We don't want that to be said of us! We can hold on to a lot in our heart. On our wholeness journey, our heart needs to be checked constantly so that it lines up with God's Word. We will become more physically and spiritually healthy when we do this.

As was mentioned in the last chapter, anything not helping us move forward needs to go. Holding on to the past and trying to relive it will keep us from moving forward. Holding on to the what-ifs and what could have been will keep us from moving forward. Looking at what everyone else has and comparing ourselves to them will keep us from moving forward. Every day, we must ask God to help us keep wrong things out of our heart. We also need to make sure we are not surrounding ourselves with people or are in environments where those wrong thoughts can come up and grow in our hearts. Our heart and mind do connect and affect each other. What is on the inside of our heart will eventually show up on the outside. Our behavior and attitudes will reveal what is in our heart. That is why it is so important that we keep out revenge, unforgiveness, complaining, jealousy, and comparison among other things. Do not forget to check the corners and little parts that may get overlooked.

      What we hold in our heart is like treasure. A treasure is special and has high value. Let us make sure we have good treasure in our heart. At the beginning part of Matthew 12:35, it says, "A good man out of the good treasure of his heart brings forth good things." I do not know about you, but I want good things to come out of my heart! That is why the state of our spiritual heart is just as important as our physical heart. God wants to help us get the bad treasure out quickly. If it lingers too long, there could be severe consequences. Love, peace, joy, thankfulness, forgiveness, kindness, humility, and faithfulness are the good treasures we want found in our heart and will add to us becoming whole. When these are found in the inside of our heart, they will help us on our journey to wholeness.

Chapter 4

The Time Is Now

So teach us to number our days, that we may gain a heart of wisdom. Psalm 90:12

"Yesterday is history, tomorrow is a mystery, today is a gift of God, which is why we call it the present." – Bill Keane

      Twenty -four hours. That's how much time we are all given in a day. I know sometimes it doesn't feel like it's that much time though! About 7 or 8 of those hours should be spent sleeping. Another 7-8 hours are spent at work or school. How are you spending the rest of the hours? How are you using that time? Watching television, on social media, cooking, spending time with family or outdoors? Each day we live to see is special and should not be taken for granted. The way we use our time on our journey to wholeness is important. Seeing and talking to the people we see every day is important. We should not take them for granted. We should appreciate having conversation with others as much as possible. We never know when it will be the last conversation we have with them. Once an opportunity is gone, we may not be able to get that opportunity back again. Once a day is gone, we can't get that day back again. Now every minute of our day does not need to be filled with us being "busy." Becoming whole does involve productivity, but it also involves knowing when to slow down. Being productive is good, but we also don't want to wear ourselves out either! At some point in the day, we should take the opportunity to rest and relax. It's okay to leave space in our day to do nothing. I'm learning this more and more! We need those moments to be refreshed and renewed.

     Every moment we live on our journey counts. It's not the time to give up. It's not the time to complain, criticize, or compare. It's not the time to be rude and jealous. It's not the time to gossip and think we're better than others. It's not the time to be silent about things that really matter. It's not the time to go backwards. Now is the time to go forward. It's time to set a good example. It's time to pray. It's time to listen and learn. It's time to be kind and appreciate what you have. It's time to forgive and love others. It's time to do the best you can and look out for others. It's time to treat everyone the same regardless of their physical appearance. It's time to speak up about what really matters. It's time to unite and stand together for what's right. The time is now. We can't put off tomorrow what we can do today. Let's be determined to use our time wisely and make every moment count towards wholeness. The time is now!

Chapter 5

How Well Do You Know Yourself?

What's your favorite color? food? sport to watch or play? game to play? What type of books do you like to read? What types of movies do you like to watch? What music do you like to listen to? What are your likes and dislikes? Are you more of an outdoors person or an indoors person? What are your strengths and weaknesses? Who is your role model and why? These are questions we should be able to answer about ourselves. A lot to think about, right?! Before we talk about getting to know others on our journey, we must get to know ourselves. You see, God knows us very well! He knows every detail about our lives. Psalm 139:1 tells us that God has searched us and knows us. He knows when we sit down, when we get up, what we're thinking and what we're going to say before we say it (v.2-4). That's not just a select few, but everyone in the whole world. That's a lot of people! That's awesome! That also means that while others may not know what we're thinking or saying, God does. We must be mindful of what we do and where we go because God is always watching. With all that is going on in our world and personal lives, God still knows it all and cares about it all. He thinks about us so much (v.17). When we think about something or someone a lot, it usually means we care about them. If God takes that much time to care about us, we should take time to care about us too.

We should appreciate who we are and who God made us to be. Before we can really appreciate others, we must first learn to appreciate who we are. The beauty of it is that our answers to the questions mentioned earlier don't have to look like everyone else's. In fact, they're not supposed to! Sure, we will have a few answers like someone else, but for the most part, they'll be different. That's perfectly okay. God loves diversity! We're different for a purpose. We all have different gifts, talents, skills, and abilities for a reason. They are all needed. With each of us using what we have and working together, it can be very beautiful and unifying. So, take some time to get to know you. It's important we know ourselves on this journey. When we meet someone for the first time and want to know more about them (singles especially, where you at?!), questions need to be asked and answered and we need to be prepared. So, let's keep learning about ourselves. Let's keep asking ourselves questions and look closely at what we want and don't want. We must ask God to search us and clear our heart out of anything not like Him (v.23). He will show us when we ask Him. We want the wrong to be replaced with something right and better. We need to embrace our uniqueness and what makes us special. When we do, we'll be able to say with the writer David in Psalm 139:14: "I will praise you, for I am fearfully and wonderfully made; Marvelous are Your works, and that my soul knows very well." Don't forget to love you. There will never be another you. We need you. You are you!

Chapter 6

That's What Friends Are For

Take a minute and think about the friends in your life right now. What makes them a friend? How would you describe them? As you think about your current friends, let me share with you what the definition of a friend is. According to the American Heritage Dictionary, a friend is defined as a person whom one knows, likes, and trusts. Does that sound like the friends you have? We should enjoy being around our friends, not dreading the time we have with them. We should be excited when we get to talk to them and hang out with them. Our friends should be supportive and encouraging to us, and we should support and encourage them as well. We should pray for our friends and want to see the best for them. They should pray for us and want to see the best for us too. If we have friends who want to see our downfall, stay stuck in the past and not get better or move forward, then they're not a friend! Friends understand that none of us are perfect, but will love us in spite of our mistakes and wrong choices. Being a friend is more than just saying it in words. It's more than saying you are friends with someone on social media. Actions always speak much louder than words!

In Mark 5:1-12 in the Bible, we see that there are 4 men who helped one of their friends who had his life changed forever. Now that's what you call real friends! In these verses, we see Jesus is teaching at a house that is packed with lots of people. In fact, there is no room left for anyone else to come in the house "not even near the door (v.2)." People were everywhere! However, there were 4 men who were determined to get their friend in that house by any means necessary. They knew Jesus was there and knew their friend's life could be changed if they could get him near Jesus. As Jesus is preaching the Word in the house, a loud noise starts to be heard. Now I'm sure the people are thinking what is that noise they keep hearing. I'm sure it caused some to look up because it sounded like the noise was coming from the roof. In fact, it sounded like the roof was about to get ripped off. Well, lo and behold, that's exactly what it was! Right before the people's very eyes, the roof had been opened and a man lying on a bed was being lowered down in the house. Now, the man lying on the bed was paralyzed and had not been able to walk. What a scene!

When Jesus saw what was happening, he stopped preaching for a moment and said two things to the man who was on the bed. First, He said, "Son, your sins are forgiven you (v.5)." Second, He said, "Arise, take up your bed, and go to your house (v.11)." Jesus spoke to him as a father would speak to a child. He spoke to him in love. He also forgives him for the wrong he had done. The man had not told Jesus he had done anything wrong. Up to this point, the man hasn't said a word! But Jesus knew, just like He knows about us. Jesus forgave the man and released him from any shame or guilt he had. Also, take note that Jesus addressed the man's spiritual state before he addressed his physical state. Once the man had faith to believe he was forgiven and worthy of love, then he could have faith to believe he could physically walk, which leads to the second thing Jesus said. Jesus told him to get up, pick up the very bed he was lying on and go home. This required faith on the man's part since he did not come in the house walking on his own. Well, his faith and Jesus' healing power showed up in a big way! In front of everyone, the man immediately got up, took up his bed and walked out on his own for all to see (v.12). What a great miracle!

Now let's go back for a minute and talk about the four men who brought their friend to Jesus. They wanted to see their friend's condition change. You see, real friends see us down, but don't want us to stay down. They encourage us and want to see us rise above whatever is trying to keep us down. They want to see us move forward. Real friends will be there for us no matter what the situation. They are not afraid to tell us the truth in love and will not let us settle for less than the best. They don't want to see us being mistreated or taken advantage of. They will stand with us through the thick and thin, through the good and bad. We need people who are good for our mental health and that will not drain us. We need people that can pour into us and we can pour into them.

Today, check your friend circle. How does it look? Don't get discouraged by the number. I've learned it's better to have a few faithful friends than a whole lot who claim to be friends in name only. Over time, we may lose friends and that's okay. It hurts, but God will send who you need to be a part of the journey. Some people are with us for certain seasons, while others may be with us for a longer time. Can you count and depend on the friends you currently have? Can they count and depend on you as a friend? Don't take your friends for granted. Appreciate and value them greatly. I want to say a big thank you to all my friends! Your support, presence and help mean so much to me! Your encouragement helps me continue to press on. Real friends know that there's more ahead for us and that we should keep going. Keep going on this wholeness journey, my friend!

Chapter 7

Half Empty or Half Full?

When it comes to life, you may have heard this question asked before: "Do you see the glass half empty or half full?" Now, I have heard this question many times. When I first heard the question, I thought that I'm a positive person and try to look on the bright side of things, so I would answer with the glass half full. But then I saw a quote more recently that challenged my thinking. The quote talked about how it doesn't matter if you see the glass half empty or half full, but that the glass is refillable. I thought, "Wow! I never thought of it that way before!" It changed my whole perspective on that question. I see the glass representing our body. The Bible talks about in I Corinthians 6:19-20 how our body is a temple and that we should honor God with our body. We honor God with our body by taking care of it. We watch what we put in it. We watch what we do with it. We make sure that it doesn't break down. Burnout can happen quickly to all ages! We all can do too much and overextend ourselves. It's a daily process to know what we can and cannot do, which I'm constantly learning. We can't take on everything because it gets too heavy.

Have you ever tried walking with a glass of water that was full and very close to the top? You hoped no one stopped you or bumped into you. You didn't want to trip before getting to your destination. One wrong move and there's a spill! Now let's imagine the glass does spill. If the water hits the floor, that could be a major problem because someone could slip and fall. Someone needs to mop it up and put wet floor signs out, so people can be cautious in that area. Now if the water hits the sink, bathtub, or plant, then the water spilling over in it would be fine. Those are designed to hold water. To review, remember the glass represents our body. The water represents what we put in our bodies. Food and drink goes in our bodies, but so do other things we may not think of right away. What television shows, movies, music, and podcasts are you listening to? What social media posts and videos are you taking in? What we consume and take in definitely fills us up.

    Just like the actual glass can get full and tends to spill out, we too can spill out things. If the right things come out and go to the right place, it's okay. However, if it's wrong things, people can slip and fall, and it could be a dangerous situation. What comes out of us does affect others and ourselves. Here's something else to think about. What if the water in that glass never got a refill? Physically, we need to keep drinking water and get refills so we don't get tired, dehydrated, and weak. In our lives, we can't keep pouring out to others and not be filled up ourselves. Colossians 3:16 tells us the Word of God should be in us, along with spiritual songs and psalms. All are based in God's truth. We also need to get rest. Our bodies get tired! Our mind, along with our physical body, can also get tired. We must constantly check our mind for thoughts that can drain us and have us all over the place. That's where our refill comes in. We need to be refreshed and renewed. We need to be refueled, be still, and get our rest. We can't pour into anyone else if we're empty. There needs to be a healthy balance of pouring into ourselves and pouring into others, which I'm working on all the time. What are we pouring out to others? Let's make sure it's not negativity, drama, hostility, gossip, or selfishness. Instead, let's pour kindness, love, truth, encouragement, compliments, thankfulness, hope into others, and ourselves. We should watch and listen to things that feed the positive and not negative.

So, it goes back to the question at the beginning- Half empty or half full? It's neither really, but the key is to observe how we feel, what we're giving, what we take in and make sure there's a healthy balance of the two. Healthy balance is what the wholeness journey is all about. As we look out for others, let's remember to look out for ourselves and refill. We can refill as often and as much as we need to. After all, when we fill up with good things, we're helping others and ourselves on this wholeness journey!

Chapter 8

Red Light, Green Light

Does the game come to your mind when you first see this title? Most, if not all of us, have played or watched this game being played at some point. Maybe it's been a long time since you played the game, or maybe you have played it more recently! This game has been played numerous times by people of all ages. A side note for parents and anyone that takes care of kids: Red Light, Green Light is an easy, fun way to get everyone up and moving! In the game, red means to stop and green means to go. As one person stands in front of the others and calls out red or green, the people playing must listen very carefully. One moves forward or stands still according to what is being said. In other words, you must listen to the directions. If you don't listen carefully, you might keep going when you're supposed to stop or stop when you're supposed to go! With that thought, let's look at the Scripture, II Timothy 3:16. It says, "All Scripture is given by inspiration of God, and is profitable for doctrine, for reproof, for correction, for instruction in righteousness." The Word of God will direct and teach us what's right and wrong. It tells us the "red lights" and "green lights" to watch out for in our lives and the world around us. God's Word gives us instructions and will not lead us to do something wrong. However, just like in the game, we must listen closely to what is being said and act accordingly.

In our lives, there are red lights that we need to be aware of and stop before we find ourselves doing them. One red light we should look out for is selfishness. When we're selfish, it becomes all about us. Now don't get me wrong...we do need to be our best, look our best, and take care of ourselves the best way possible. But when it becomes all about you all the time and that's it, there's a problem. Sometime during our day, we should think about how we can help, encourage or give a compliment to someone else. Let's not get so caught up in what we have going on that we miss the opportunity to check on or help somebody else. Another red light we need to watch out for is complaining. We need to take time in our day to be thankful for what and who we still have in our lives. We should be thankful for the health and strength God has given us. We need to remember that things could be worse than what they are right now. Making a list of what you're thankful for or writing the items down on note cards can help remind you of what you have to be thankful for. Another red light to watch out for is worry. This is one I have to constantly work on in my personal life. The minute we start to worry, we have put our focus on the problem and not on God. When the thoughts of worry come, we need to pray and take a deep breath. Start walking around or doing something constructive (listen to music, draw, exercise) to get your mind off what is worrying you. There's more "red lights,", but I just mentioned a few of them here. When we see these red lights, we need to hit the brakes and stop. We need to turn away from them and not participate in them. They can't come with us on the wholeness journey.

On the other hand, there are "green lights" that we should go and do. We should learn the lessons from our past and move on. We should learn all we can and use it when we can. We should pray, spend time with God and other believers. We should love, be kind, help others, forgive, and be thankful. Now you may be thinking- "Isn't there a color we're missing?!" You're right. There is another light I haven't mentioned yet. It's the yellow traffic light and it means to slow down. There are things in our lives that we need to be cautious and slow to do. Some of us have rushed into things or said things too quick! When we're rushing, we can make wrong decisions. James 1:19 in the Bible talks about "yellow lights" that we need to look out for. In that verse, it talks about being slow to speak and slow to becoming angry. We can't say the first thing we think of (which is not always easy!). Let's pray first and think before we speak or do something we may later regret. As we go about our daily lives, we must pay attention and be alert to the signs because the lights can change quickly. We need to totally rely on God and know God's Word to help us through those changes. Let's follow God's Word and act accordingly every day. Remember that God's directions will never lead us wrong. As you proceed in life, remember to keep an eye on the signs, so we can stay on God's path.

Chapter 9

Likes, Comments, Follows

To like or not like? To comment or not comment? To follow or not follow? If you've ever been on social media for any amount of time (or know someone who is), then these questions may sound very familiar. If not, welcome to the world of social media! Over the years, there has been an increase in social media use. Especially with everything that went on with the pandemic in the past few years, social media was a main way for people to meet, communicate, keep in touch, stay up to date with news, and attend meetings and events online. On any given day, many posts and messages flood our timeline in a matter of minutes. As we're scrolling through the posts, we have a choice to make. We can stop and read it or keep scrolling past it. If we do stop to read it, we then have another choice. We can like it, love it, comment, or do none of them. We may just read it and move on.

Is it okay to not respond to every post we see? Absolutely yes! It doesn't mean we didn't see it or read it. Then, we have a choice of whether to follow a certain page or send/accept a friend request. Just because it's presented to us doesn't mean we have to accept or follow back. If it's not feeding your spirit in a positive way or uplifting you in any way, then it needs to be a no. I'm learning not to follow everything and stay away from drama, negativity, and toxicity. I'm also learning to stay away from things that will feed comparison as I know that's something I've struggled with. If it makes me uneasy and causing me to think wrong, I don't need to go there.

When choosing what to like, comment and follow, use wisdom (James 1:5) and make the right choice for you.

Be sincere and have right motives. Don't follow and like just because everybody else is or to compete with someone else. Comments should be sincere and relevant to what the message is about. On the other side of this, we can't get caught up in how many likes, follows, and comments our posts get or don't get. The number of likes on our posts does not determine our worth. The number of follows we have does not determine how loved we are. In fact, here's a secret (or maybe not so much!): everyone who follows or like your posts does not want the best for you. Some do and some don't. Some want to truly see how you're doing and are encouraged by what you post. Others are waiting for you to fall or fall apart. In other words, not everyone has right motives. That's alright though!

My encouragement to you: keep posting messages that are positive and helpful because you never know who is reading them. Whether you get 1 like, 100 likes or no likes, what matters is that you share hope with others. What matters is that you send encouragement and shine light on situations that seem dim and discouraging. One post could change someone's whole life! The likes, comments and follows can be good, but that's not what makes you or others amazing. We are amazing apart from all of that! I'm constantly reminding myself not to get caught up in who liked my post, how many likes (or loves or cares in Facebook's case) my posts get, and how come it didn't get any or a few likes. My worth is not in numbers, and neither is yours. My hope is not in numbers and yours shouldn't be either. My worth and hope is in God alone. So, likes, comments, and follows can all be good when viewed in a healthy manner. Let's choose wisely. Let's post wisely. Let's like, comment, and follow wisely. Let's choose to make a positive change one post at a time.

Chapter 10

Lessons From the Mountains

Peaceful. Breathtaking. Relaxing. Stunning. Beautiful. Appreciative. These are just a few words I would use to describe my trip to the mountains in 2021. One of my cousins and I had the wonderful opportunity to visit Massanutten, Virginia for a beautiful, fall weekend in October. It was our first time visiting Massanutten, and it definitely won't be our last. In fact, it was my first time ever visiting the mountains on a vacation! I loved every minute of it! The closer we got to our destination, the more excited we became. The vacation was a much-needed break to be still and reset, refocus, and readjust. It was also a great reminder to enjoy life and be thankful for the opportunities that come my way to do so. As I was in the mountains, I learned a lot of lessons and I want to share some of them here with you:

1. <u>Soak up every minute of every day</u>. It is important to be present and enjoy every minute life brings. The mountains were so beautiful, and I didn't want to miss seeing anything! From sightseeing to watching movies to shopping to laughs, we never had a dull moment. We embraced every opportunity to learn and have fun!
2. <u>Appreciate and spend time with your loved ones who are still here with you</u>. In losing lots of my loved ones over time, I learned this lesson early on in my life, but the trip reminded me once again. Spending time with my cousin was the best! It was the first vacation I had taken since my Mom passed. I did have bittersweet moments thinking about how she wouldn't see me off on my trip and wouldn't be home when I got back. I wasn't able to tell her about

my trip, but I did tell my brother about it. At the same time, I thought about how she would have been proud of me navigating the mountains with my cousin. Several times, my cousin and I talked about my Mom. One time, I said something my Mom would have said. My cousin said you sound just like her and then we had a good laugh. I thought about how my Mom and Dad both would have loved it there as neither one of them got a chance to visit there. While we were on the trip, my cousin and I checked in with loved ones back at home every day. We never know when it will be our last time, so every moment needs to be used wisely.

3. <u>Take lots of pictures!</u> Now I know, for some of you, this may be stepping out of your comfort zone. Try it sometime though. Take pictures of your loved ones and the scenery around you. You don't always have to go to the mountains to take pictures as there are opportunities all around us. It doesn't take much for my cousin and I to take pictures. Before we got to our hotel, we stopped to take pictures. We had a whole photoshoot going! We didn't waste any time! You should have seen us. We were like children at Christmas time- I loved it! The fall leaves changing was absolutely beautiful. We were in a new place and wanted to capture it all.

4. <u>Try new things</u>. It doesn't matter how big or small it may seem. A small step out of your comfort zone is better than no step forward at all. Going to a new place itself was a win for me! Then, while I was there, I had new experiences, saw new sights, and went to new stores and restaurants. It felt good to do that and I need to do that more often.

5. <u>Be still.</u> Reset and refocus. This is one I am constantly working on and have to remind myself of

often. We don't always have to be doing something. It's okay to sit still. I remember that the Saturday we were there it rained, so we stayed in more. As I was relaxing in our hotel room, I told my cousin that I don't do this much. I definitely need to be still more. It is important that our bodies get rest and refuel. Our bodies were created to get rest and not always be on the move. There is a time to do each and there needs to be a balance of the two. Being still was also so peaceful and serene. It was perfect!

Maybe you can't visit the mountains or go on a vacation soon. That's okay. You can still embrace new opportunities. You can still try new things. You can still be appreciative of who and what you have in your life. You see, a lovely gem tucked away in Virginia called Massanutten was just what I needed to reignite my faith and focus on this wholeness journey. I am forever grateful. Here's to new beginnings !!

Chapter 11

Who's Calling?

Accept or decline? Most of us see these two buttons when a call comes on our cell phone. The accept button is green and the decline button is red. In the terms of the traffic lights mentioned in a previous chapter, green is associated with go and red is associated with stopping. When we see a phone call come through, we have two choices. We can either accept the call or decline the call. In other words, we can answer the call or not answer it. If you have caller ID, the name and phone number will appear. If they are in your contact list on your cell phone, their name (person or organization) will display. If it's a spam call, it will usually be labeled as potential spam. Oh the beauty of caller ID! The caller ID allows us to see who wants our attention on the other side of the call. Then, there are the times when someone will call you and you don't recognize the phone number. It could be someone you know that is not in your contacts or they are using someone else's phone. They could have also gotten a new number, which is another reason why you may not recognize the contact. If we don't recognize the number at first, we can usually identify quick if it's someone you know based on their voice and information they're saying on the other end if you answer it. We can also ask questions to better know who's on the other end.

A while back, I was riding with a family member heading to a family function. Her phone rang while we were riding. She looked at the display to see the name of the person and declined to answer. Well, the same person called back again, and she responded the same way. She hit decline. At the moment, it had to be delayed as she didn't have time for what the person on the other end was going to say because she knew from previous conversations what was going to be said. She did call another family member and shared with them the situation, so it was handled. It was in that moment it hit me! We don't have to answer everything that wants our attention. Think back to what I said earlier about how someone calling wants our attention. There are many things in life that want our attention, but we have the choice whether we respond and how we respond if we do.

In the Scriptures in Colossians 3:5-9, it tells us things we should not answer to. Things that will cause us to act and live impure, selfish, greedy, tell lies, and speak wrong words should not be accepted. In Romans 12:9, 14-19, it tells us more things we should not respond to, but it also includes what we should respond to. The verses tell us not to respond with pride (v.16), revenge (v.17, 19) or evil with evil (v.21). Instead, we should only answer to what is being done in love (see I Corinthians 13:4-7 that describes love in action) and engage in peaceful interactions. We should not answer to anything that goes against what God's Word says. To know what it says, we must take time to study and read the Scriptures for ourselves. Knowing the Word will help us keep it stored in our hearts and help us not do wrong, so we can stay on the path of God's commands (Psalms 119:11, 35). When we have the Word in us, we're more likely to decline anything that will waste our time. Now there is a time to answer and respond to the phone calls that come from our family, friends, work, community, and medical offices to take care of what is needed. You may be able to answer the call right then. You may have to wait and delay it until later like my cousin did that day during the car ride. In the case of a spam call or someone you don't know, you may not answer the call at all.

    In our lives, we need to be wise in what and who we allow to be in our lives. When seeing what wants our attention, we have to check the source before we answer. If we don't know at first, let's ask, "Who's calling?" A response or a lack of a response will help us decide our next steps. Decline and say "bye" to the things that leave us feeling drained, exhausted, and on the wrong path. Let's say "hello" to things that lead us to peace, love, knowing our value, and on the right path. We get to choose every day what we will accept or decline on our life journey. Remember to choose wisely because the choice is ours!!

Chapter 12

Practice the Pause

Imagine you are in the middle of watching a movie or you're listening to a song or podcast and you're really into it. Then, all of a sudden, your phone rings, someone calls your name, you hear sounds, or you have to get up for something. Maybe, you were even watching a video on YouTube, and it stops because the Internet service has been interrupted. When that happens, there has been a pause. A pause happens when an action is interrupted briefly. We all have experienced a pause before whether it was in our control or not. Notice that a pause is not a permanent action. It will continue later. Now whether that's one minute later or one hour later, it will begin again. I will say that a pause can be frustrating or disappointing (especially if you were at a really good part of what you're watching!). It doesn't mean you won't ever get to see it, but now you must wait.

Videos aren't the only thing that have been put on pause before. Goals can be put on pause. There can be a pause in conversations in person or on the phone. There can be moments in our day where we pause and be still. In looking at the examples above, we can all relate to at least one of them when we're thinking about the pause. I've learned that a pause is not necessarily bad and could be a good thing. It may not always be convenient, but we can learn in the pause. We can rest and regroup in the pause. A pause is when something is still and absent of movement. I took a communication class in my undergraduate studies program in college. In the class, we discussed the importance of having pauses in our conversation. We talked about how in our society we always feel like we need to fill the silence in conversation and not have the pause. However, we learned that the pause is okay. Silence is okay. It allows those involved to think about what is being said and not rush what needs to be communicated. I try to remind myself of that when I'm having conversations even though I still get the urge to want to fill the silence. This happens especially when the conversation is getting really good, and I want to jump in right away!

Sometimes, we have to pause in pursuing our goals. I had to practice the pause when I was pursuing my Master's degree. I started working on it in September 2017. I was planning to complete it in 3 years by 2020. Notice I said "I." God had other plans. In 2019, I had to take a pause with going to school. I only had one more course to take and that was the student teaching credit. I was very close to finishing! In the pause, I kept working at the school with my Reading students and learned all I could in my classroom experiences. I picked my goal back up in January 2021 and completed my Master's degree in Elementary Education in April 2021! Yes, I had to take a pause, but I didn't quit. I didn't give up on my goal. Oh yes... I do need to mention that I took one class at a time! I want to stop right here and encourage those of you who are currently going to school or college and it seems like it's taking forever for you to finish. Keep going and keep taking those classes, even if you have to take one class at a time. You will reach your goal! Slow and steady wins the race- I am living proof!!

So, let's practice the pause. In our conversations, let's have a few moments of silence. James 1:19 in the Bible tells us to be slow to speak. Allow for the pause before the next words are spoken. In the pause, we can make sure we are responding in the right way with the right attitude. Let's practice the pause in prayer so we can hear any instructions and Scriptures God needs to tell and remind us of. If there is a goal you have had to pause on, keep going and do the best you can. It will come to pass. We can take a break from that project or task we've been doing to go outside, read our book, go to a spa or salon, or do something we enjoy. It's okay to pause from the action. Sometimes we should go back to it the same day, while other times we should wait until another day. In each day itself, let's just sit in silence for a few moments. Let's not worry about the to-do list, what we need to do later or what we should be doing while we're sitting there. These are real thoughts and easier to say than do (trust me- I'm with you!), but let's keep working on that. Every day, let's practice the pause in our words and actions. Then, whenever we're ready, we can hit "Play!" and resume!!

Chapter 13

Time to Switch!

Transitions are all around us. Transitions are changes from one phase or state to another. Changes happen in our communities, churches, schools, colleges, personal lives, and the world around us. Changes are not always comfortable. Some changes we see coming, while others are very unexpected. In our lives, we see the human development of a baby to a toddler to school-age to pre-teen to teen to adulthood. At each level, something new is required as our responsibilities change. For example, a toddler will not be expected to do what a teenager does. When students reach a certain age in school, they begin to switch (or change) classes. They don't stay in the same classroom all day, but they must move to different classrooms. With the transition comes adjustments and learning new habits and routines.

As a sixth grade English teacher, I see firsthand how students transition to different classes in person. I have also seen the effect of the online learning since the pandemic. It was a big adjustment for students and teachers to go from virtual to in-person! What I haven't shared with you yet is that I am in my third year teaching a core subject. I love it and am adjusting all the time! I'm grateful for all the experiences leading up to now because they taught me flexibility. I've had to adjust to being responsible for more students, more paperwork, more meetings to attend, and more emails. I went from working with a smaller group of students in specialized Reading instruction to teaching a whole grade level English. Whew! A transition indeed! Let's also not forget a pandemic was going on during the transition. I am learning so much and am growing through everything. I'm thankful for the knowledge I can share, and I hope it is encouraging to others!

The transition in my career was expected as I was looking for a classroom teaching position after getting my Master's degree in 2021. Praise God for that! In addition to my career transition, there's been the transition in my relationships. God knows who and what I need in this season as far as friendships. When it comes to dating, I only want the best and not settle out of desperation or loneliness for just any guy. I've been praying that God remove anyone out of my life that is not His best for me. I'm also learning not to assume anything, but ask questions and communicate about everything, whether big or small. I have been disappointed with that and assumed things I shouldn't have in the past, but I learned my lesson there. It's a transition period and I'm learning to be okay with it. There are days I wonder what is going on in the dating scene, but I know God sees what's ahead. I've come a long way and continue to grow in Him in this area.

Then, in 2020 (January 18th, 2020 to be exact), I had one of the biggest transitions of my life. It was a transition that was unexpected. It was the day I transitioned to being a daughter who had both parents pass away. My Dad passed away in April 2002 and my Mom passed away on January 18, 2020. It's a transition that's still hard to believe. My brother and I have had to adjust in the household without our parents. We are growing and being blessed! I am adjusting to sitting in the living room and not seeing them sitting there (especially Momma laid back in the recliner or in her favorite spot on the couch and them not sitting at their spots at the dining room table!). I've had to adjust to going to church and Momma not sitting beside me there. Every now and then, I peep down at the seat she liked to sit on in the middle near the aisle. I do go to church with one of my aunts now and I enjoy our aunt- niece time together! I've had to adjust not being able to share everything going on with my parents. However, I'm grateful for what I did share with them, and those God has currently placed in my life I can share with. You all know who you are and you are the best! So, you know how I said earlier that 6th grade students switch classes? Well, that was another big adjustment for me: the schedule when they switched. You have to memorize the time. In my first year of teaching, I missed it a lot and would go over a few minutes! I would hear the students in the hallway and that helped me remember it was time to switch. I have the time down now. I must teach while also being mindful of the time and when it's time to switch.

    In life, we must be sensitive to God's leading when it's time to switch. We may not think we're ready, but God has been preparing us for the moment whether we realize it or not. I was being prepared to be the English teacher I am now. I was being prepared to navigate life without my parents. I was being prepared for this single season I'm currently in. I am being prepared for my future marriage as I believe there is a God-sent man who will love and appreciate me for me. Through all our transitions, we must remember that God never changes (Malachi 3:6). We must let Him lead in all things (Psalms 32:8). Life will always be full of transitions. The key is to learn, embrace and grow with each one. It's all part of the journey to wholeness. Then when it's time to switch, let's keep growing and glowing!

Chapter 14

Bounce Back

We all have setbacks. We all have disappointments. We all have experienced rejection. We all have been hurt in some way or another. It's not fun. It's not easy. It can be hard to look up again, to trust again, to move forward. In fact, it can be downright devastating. I have good news today- we can bounce back!! It doesn't happen all at once or overnight, but it will happen. As I mentioned in the last chapter, my Mom passed away in January 2020 after a brief illness. In our house, my brother and I have plants from before my Mom passed and after she passed. Her plants skills must have rubbed off on us because the plants that were blooming when she was here are still blooming! The plants we have in our house are lily plants. I love them! Side note: If you're looking for an easy house plant to take care of, lilies are what you want! We have two lily plants - one was here when our Mom was here and one came along after her. Our oldest lily plant has been with us since 2008! The leaves on the lily plant droop when it needs water. Now the lilies don't need to be watered every day, but I love how they let you know what they need. The leaves drooping is their signal saying "Water me."

When it droops, there is no need to throw it away or stop watering it. It just needs attention. Just because it's down doesn't mean it's dead- a Word for somebody! While we have a nice amount of house plants, we didn't have a lot of outside flowers. So, back in 2021, my brother and I purchased two outdoor flowers. One sat in our backyard and was called new guinea. It bloomed beautifully in the season we had it in. The other flower, the petunia, sat in our front yard. The petunia started off doing well, but then I noticed after a week or so, it wasn't flourishing like the new guinea. Did you see how I was comparing the two?! I mean, I saw a few flower petals, but not as many as when we first got the flower. Then, lo and behold, about 2 weeks after that, all the flower petals were gone! Both my brother and I noticed it. One day when I was watering the new guinea, I walked by the petunia and said I'm going to water it. Now remember at this point, there were no flower petals. There was no evidence whatsoever. It may have looked crazy to someone else, but I watered it anyway because I knew it had the potential to bounce back. Now go with me about a week later. I was outside and looked at the petunia again. Guess what I saw this time?! Flower petals! That's right- they had bounced back!

    In that moment, God taught me a lesson. We don't have to be worried. We don't have to compare our growth to others. Both the new guinea and petunia were beautiful in their own way. It is the same way with us as individuals. We are uniquely beautiful in our own way. Our wholeness journey doesn't have to look like everyone else's. We may not be blooming as fast as the next person, but we need to trust God for our timing. I have felt like the late bloomer with a lot of things, but that's alright. God is truly growing me and I'm thankful! Just because you don't see evidence right away with your physical eyes doesn't mean change isn't happening. We can't stop praying. We can't stop serving. We can't stop being consistent. Are we watering and taking care of the seeds we already have? Will we still serve even when we don't see results? Will we still love even when others are not treating us right? Will we still help even when it seems like no one is helping us? Will we still pray even when we haven't seen an answer? Will we still stand and speak God's promises even when we haven't seen it unfold fully, but we know it will? Will you be like the petunia and bounce back? Keep doing all the things you know to do. Do them well. Do them consistently. Do them faithfully. Do them wholeheartedly. Before you know it, you'll see a sprout here and a sprout there and then a whole flower petal. And, not just one, but several! So, it's not too late- we can bounce back!

Chapter 15

Nothing Hidden

"Peek-a-boo, I see you." Do you remember playing that game back in the day as a little kid or with little kids you have or know? My Mom used to babysit a lot of kids over the years. I remember my Mom and I playing that game with them all the time. I like to say she babysat the whole community because she really did. Shout out to all the kids that you used to hang out with us! If you're reading this, I love you and appreciate you!! To see their faces light up and laugh when we would cover our eyes and then uncover them in this game was pure joy. They couldn't see our eyes at first as we held our hands in front of them. Sometimes, we would slowly pretend like we were uncovering our eyes and then cover them back real quick. The laughs that my Mom and children had were the absolute best with them! It was so much fun- those were the days I will forever cherish. In the game, only your eyes stay covered for a little before they see them. Then the hiding game steps up when you get older with hide and seek. In hide and seek, one person counts to a certain number while everyone else goes to hide. After the person has finished counting, then they go to "seek" everyone else who has hidden. No longer is it just your eyes that are covered, but it's the whole body now. The people intentionally hide their whole body, so they can't be found easily by the person who was doing the seeking. In both games described above, some part or all of you are hiding from the view of others.

Now these are just games being played, but sometimes (a lot of times if we're honest!), we hide in real life. To hide means not to be seen and out of view of others. In life, we hide our problems, talents, skills, opinions, and personality from others. We may not want anyone to know something is wrong and let them believe everything is fine. We may have a certain skill or talent that we keep hidden from others. We may not want people to know our real likes and dislikes or opinions about a certain issue because they may not accept us or want us in their friend circle. We may hide the "real" us because we're afraid of what people may say or think. Now, I agree that we should not tell everything to everybody. However, there should be a few trusted people in our circle that we can tell our problems to. No one's perfect as we all have some issues going on in our lives. Chances are that someone may be going through the exact same problem you are, but hasn't said anything. They may be relieved to know they are not alone! I heard someone refer to the people we can share with as our safety circle. These are the people that we know our problem is safe with and will point us in the right direction with support, encouragement, and resources. By the way, if those who you call a friend can't accept you for you, then you need to find new friends! We shouldn't need to hide the real us just to be accepted.

You know who else we don't have to hide from?! God! He sees everyone and everything going on in the world all at the same time. Proverbs 15:3 says in the Bible that his eyes are everywhere seeing the evil and good. In Psalms 139 in the Bible, David talks about how God has searched us and knows us. He sees it all and nothing is hidden. The light and darkness are all the same to God (v.12)! Since He knows everything, we don't have to hide anything from Him. We don't have to hide our problems or concerns, but we can tell Him all about it. Psalms 55:22 says we can give our burden to the Lord and that He will keep us. That's so good to know!! We don't have to hide the "real" us from Him. After all, He created us and we were not hid from Him at all (Psalms

139:15-16). We don't have to hide our gifts or talents, but we can use them to serve God and others. We are needed! We must use the gifts we've been given wisely (I Peter 4:10, Romans 12:6-8). What we can do is needed in our part of the world God has placed us in. So, there's no need to hide. When we seek Him, God will make it clear who should and shouldn't be in our life. Remember, you and all you have to offer are needed and don't need to hide. When we're in our safety circle, we can share sincerely and openly. We most certainly don't have to hide from God either. We can share what's in our heart with Him. Isn't that good news?! No "peek-a-boo" or "hide and seek" required!!

Chapter 16

Up Close and Personal

When you want to take a real good look at a room or item, you view it from every possible angle. You may even use a tool, such as a magnifying glass or a microscope, to help you see something more clear. At first glance, it may look okay. But, after careful inspection, you see details and cracks that may not be obvious at first. As I mentioned in a previous chapter, I am a teacher. During the first week back, there is a lot of unpacking and cleaning that needs to be done in the classroom. In my unpacking last year, I had one particular crate that I had taken items out of. At the bottom of the crate, there was a small crack. Now the crack wasn't huge, but it was big enough to notice if you got close to it. It was big enough that I didn't want to use it to put any items in. After all, that was the purpose of the crate. So, I put it in the hallway and labeled it as trash because I couldn't use it anymore.

Just like that crate had to be inspected, our lives need to be inspected as well. We all need to take a good look at our lives. At first glance, that crate may have looked okay to someone walking by it in the hallway. But upon closer inspection, it was not okay. We all have areas in our lives that have cracks and places that have been broken. We need to find out what they are and acknowledge them. Some things need to be totally discarded out of our lives (like the crate), while others need to be fixed. We must know the difference. To know the difference, we must pray and ask God for wisdom (James 1:5). Then, we need to stay alert and look up close and personal to see what's really going on. We can ask ourselves the question: Is it worth holding on to? I didn't need to hold on to the cracked one. If what we're holding on to and carrying is not helping us, we don't need to hold on to it.

     Now, let's take it a step further. What have we let in the cracks of our heart? Take a close look and then decide what you will do. Action must be taken. We can't let it sit there if it's not useful. Yes, I probably could have set items that were light in that crate, but eventually if enough items were weighed down in it, the crack would have gotten bigger. I knew I had the other crate and other storage items in my classroom, so I was good. We have to know what we have. What's in our life? Who's in our life? How are we using what we have? Can we even use what we have? Let's examine the cracks of anxiety, doubt, low self-esteem, pride, negativity, disrespect and see how they can be dealt with and replaced with something healthy. On the other hand, let's take love, humility, peace, confidence, and thankfulness and see how they can be seen in our lives. Let's remember to look at our life up close and personal every day. We have to make sure our heart is holding the right things and get help to let go of what we need to. We also need help in mending what we do keep. So..what do you say...It's time to get up close and personal!!

Chapter 17

Don't Settle

At some point in your life, you may have asked the question (or were asked the question): Are you all settled in now? This may have been in reference to moving to a new place, such as a house or dormitory room. In my case, it was three years ago that I moved into a new classroom. You may have also heard it being referred to when someone has a new job. In these cases, the word settle can be defined as taking residence in or to come to rest in. When we settle in somewhere, we become adjusted and acquainted with our surroundings. Settling can be a good thing, but we also don't want to get too comfortable that we are not open to new opportunities or a new way of doing something. We need to remain teachable, keep learning, and know there is always more. Ecclesiastes 3:1 tells us that, "There is an occasion for everything, and a time for every activity under heaven." We don't have to settle for the wrong. We don't have to settle for the wrong attitudes and thought patterns. We don't have to settle for wrong relationships when dating because it seems like no one else will come along, and we don't want to be lonely. We don't have to settle in hanging out with a certain group of friends because we don't think we can find anyone else to be our friend. We don't have to do it. God doesn't want us to settle in this wholeness journey.

I'm constantly reminding myself not to settle because God wants the best for me and I should too. For too long, I settled for wrong relationships when it came to dating. While I haven't dated a lot of guys, I hold tight to the past lessons I learned. A few years ago, there was one relationship that I knew I had no business even opening the door for the possibility of dating the guy. He was tied to a previous relationship, yet I talked to him anyway. I knew I was settling and should not have. The guy was nice, but had a lot of baggage and was not for me. After about two months, I had to cut that off because I did not have peace about it at all and felt like I was walking on eggshells the whole two months. More specifically, I didn't have God's peace. I remember feeling so bad about letting myself get into that relationship to begin with and feeling shameful. I remember thinking there was no hope for me in dating ever again. Thankfully, I have been able to bounce back, keep healing and move on with God's help. A side note to the ladies: don't settle for just any guy. Check his actions, motives, effort, and background. If he is coming into the relationship with baggage from a previous relationship, that is a red flag and should not be ignored. Ask questions and be honest upfront (my mistake for not doing this in the relationship I mentioned earlier). They may be nice, but not for you. Men, the same applies to you about being honest and checking those actions.

Not settling doesn't just apply in dating, but it also applies to friendships as well. If they're not treating you right, you don't have to stay in their circle. Everyone deserves to be respected and feel appreciated. If that's not happening, it's time to find a new circle. We all have settled in something. What have you been settling in? What have you been resting in lately? Maybe it is that wrong relationship or friend circle because it is a safe place, and you don't know what will happen if you let them go. Maybe you have been resting in wrong attitudes or thought patterns. Maybe you have been resting in the opinions of others or your past mistakes. Whatever you have been settling in, make sure you choose not to settle for wrong anymore. Today, we can change the course of our thoughts.

Today, we can choose our connections more wisely. We can choose to rest in God's Word today. We can choose to rest in the fact that God loves us and hasn't left us. As a matter of fact, He never will (Hebrews 13:5)! We can rest in the fact that God has more for us than what we can see right now. We can rest in the fact that God has the absolute best for us. Starting today, we can start settling in the right places with the right people!

Chapter 18

You're Almost There

Have you ever been riding somewhere and it felt like it would take forever to get there? You kept seeing signs that said the destination was a certain number of miles away and the number starts getting smaller. However, it still seemed really far away! How about your journey to become whole? How about when you've been in a race or gone hiking and it seemed like the trail or finish line would never come? Perhaps you are in school, college or professional development classes for your job and the degree or certification seems so far away. You know with every assignment turned in and every session attended that it's getting closer, yet it doesn't seem that way. Earlier this year, one of my cousins, our friend, and I went to visit High Bridge State Trail Park in Farmville, Virginia for a day trip. It's a beautiful town if you ever get a chance to visit. We walked across the bridge, which has absolutely amazing scenery! After walking across the bridge, we then decided to walk the trail underneath, so we could see underneath the bridge. Well, the 1st time we tried, we got nowhere and made one big circle!!! The second time, we tried walking on another trail. Before we got too far, a lady we saw earlier asked us were we sure we wanted to go that way because it was steep. We decided not to go on that trail and asked her to help us get to the right one. So, we tried a third time (I heard the third time's a charm!) to get on the trail. We went back to the first trail and realized we had missed the right turn down the path. Well, we saw the right trail previously, but didn't notice it. We had walked right by it! The lady got us on the right track- thank goodness!! She knew we had no idea what we were doing!! You had to be there though because we were having a wonderful time enjoying nature and laughing the whole time!!!

Once we got on the right path, we kept moving forward. Now, at several points, we wondered is this really taking us underneath the bridge. However, with every step we took, we were getting closer to our destination. We kept going! As we got closer, our friend said she could see the bridge as she was in front of my cousin and me. That's how we knew we were on the right track! Sure enough, the bridge looms in our sight. Before we knew it, we were there! It was all worth it because it was breathtaking!! To stand underneath the bridge and look up to see all the wonderful architecture was amazing!! We reached our destination because we accepted help and directions on how to get there. We didn't turn around before we got there, but we kept walking the trail even when we questioned if it looked right.

In life, there are times we want to reach goals and may attempt to reach them, but then we get distracted or turned around and don't reach the goal. I want to share some of the lessons I learned from my trip. First, take time to soak in every moment and your surroundings. Being out in nature was peaceful and calming. Sometimes, we can get so caught up in reaching our destination that we forget to enjoy the scenery along the way. Second, keep taking steps toward your goal. As we kept walking the trail, the closer we got to see the bridge from underneath. Third, keep people in your circle that will encourage you to keep going because they can see something you can't see. As we walked the trail, our friend was in front. She made the comment she could see the bridge. My cousin and I couldn't see it at first, but we kept going and then we saw it too. We need people in our lives that will tell us not to give up because they see we're almost there and we've been working too hard to give up now. Next, we need to remember our why. It's the why that keeps us going and keeps us looking up. A goal I completed last year in August is getting my gifted certification! On January 11th, 2023, I started online classes through Averett University for my gifted education certification. It was an adjustment for sure with teaching full time and taking classes again, but God truly helped me. In August of 2023, I completed that goal. Yes, it got tiring and there were days I didn't feel like doing my work. Yet, I took my breaks, and then got back up and kept going.

    I remembered my why. I remembered I don't have to limit myself in one area of education. I remembered I wanted to expand my options in the education field. I remember I have students who look up to me. I remember I have the next generation in my classroom. I remember I have people in my circle who support and encourage me. I remember I have people in my life who will help me when I ask them. I remembered it would all be worth it just like seeing under the High Bridge was worth it. We had a great time on our trip and look forward to our next adventure!! So, keep going. Don't give up on your dream and goal. It's closer in sight than you think. Keep your positive support system nearby. Laugh when you can. Ask for help when you need to. Most importantly, keep putting one foot in front of the other. You're almost there! I got this! You got this! We got this because God has us!!

Chapter 19

Get in Shape!

On a scale of 1 to 10, how well are you at taking care of your physical body? A score of 10 represents excellent and a 1 represents not at all. Would you rate yourself a 1, 10 or somewhere in between? I'm not a 1 or a 10, but I would fall somewhere around a 8. My rating is a lot higher now than it used to be as I am learning more of the importance of taking care of me. I am thankful for that! We all have to do an honest reflection of areas we need to work on. For example, I know I need to work on consistently getting 7- 8 hours a sleep each night. I know it's not consistent, but I'm working towards that goal. Getting a certain number of hours and proper rest is one way we can physically take care of our bodies. We also take care of our physical bodies by drinking water, eating healthy foods, limiting junk food and sweets, brushing and flossing our teeth, and exercising regularly. All these factors are choices that an individual makes. We choose what time we go to bed, what foods we eat or don't eat and when and how often we exercise and move our bodies. These are decisions we make daily. The decisions we make will show up in our lives. For example, keeping our teeth clean will keep food from building up. Not only that, but not taking care of our teeth properly can affect our physical health in other ways too. Lack of sleep, lots of junk food and sweets and little to no exercise can also affect our physical health in a negative way. We all have some area of improvement in that. I know I do!

To make sure we are physically healthy, we have to make sure we are making good decisions on what has been discussed earlier. When we do not make good choices, we tend to be less focused, less energetic, and tired. Our physical health should be taken seriously because it is important. Doctor and dentist appointments are necessary because the professionals can help guide us in making the right decisions and make sure we are taking the necessary tests. All these things will help get us in shape and be our best self. Not only should we get in shape physically, but spiritually, emotionally, and mentally as well. We should want to be healthy in all areas of our life. Healthy and whole are my goals and I hope they are yours too!! Not being healthy in one area can affect other areas. Just like we have to watch what food and drinks we take in (the portions as well), we have to watch what we feed our soul.

What are we taking in daily? Is it growing us or weakening us? Is it giving us energy or draining us? Is it helpful or harmful? We may not see the results of taking something harmful in right away (wrong relationships, wrong conversations, wrong social media posts, etc.), but it has a way of showing up eventually. It shows up in how we talk about ourselves and others, how we treat ourselves and others, and daily routines. The effects of eating junk food or not exercising regularly may not show up right away, but try walking and being out and about for certain period of time. You'll find out real quick that you're not in shape and have a hard time keeping up like you want to! So, we must be careful what we take in our spirit because it can weigh us down and leave us feeling drained. I Timothy 6:6 says, "But godliness with contentment is great gain." Being obedient to God's Word and remembering/speaking God's promises will bring that contentment we need. It's focusing on God's teaching, so we can live out His truths in our daily lives. Living out the truth helps us to be healthy and in spiritual shape. In I Timothy 6:7-8, it talks about being spiritually fit and training for godliness because that benefits us now and in the future. We can eat sweets from time to time, but we have to watch our portions and eat it in moderation. Social media can be "sweet" too, but we have to watch how much we take in and take it in moderation. It can be a good thing, but it can also be overwhelming and influence us negatively if we let it. It goes back to the choices. Too much negativity, confusion, chaos, and drama will leave us out of shape. Earlier, it was discussed about how we should take care of our physical health. Just like physical fitness, training for godliness requires consistency. It requires doing the right thing often and not just once a week or once a month. Here are some things I am learning we can do to stay in shape:

1. <u>Study and live God's Word daily</u>. Memorize and mediate on the Scriptures throughout the days. Live out God's Word everywhere we go.

2. <u>Pray to God daily</u>. Prayer is our connection to God, just like we stay connected to our family and friends. Talk to God about everything and let Him talk back to you. Listen to what instructions He tells you to do.

3. <u>Fill ourselves up with the Word of God</u>. We have to fill ourselves up with what's good, healthy, and helpful. Just like junk food, eating sweets only gives temporary fulfillment. We need something more solid that will sustain us in the storms of life.

4. <u>Surround ourselves with friends who encourage us to stay healthy</u>. We need to check our circle. Make sure our friends are genuine and their actions show it. I've learned that it's not about the number of friends we have, but the quality of friendships. I'm thankful for my circle I can count on.

5. <u>Check in with yourself often</u>. Ask yourself how you are really doing. Take breaks to be still and reflect on who God is

and who you are in Him (Psalms 46:10, 139:3, 14). Make changes for the better as often as you need to.

6. <u>Celebrate all your wins</u>. My wins and your wins matter equally. Take time to honor and acknowledge them along your journey. They are important and deserve to be celebrated .

No matter what happens on your journey to wholeness, keep going. We're all in this healthy journey together! Little steps each day add up to big results. I see you. I am proud of you. God is proud of you. Let's keep working on us and get in shape!!

Chapter 20

Hello 40!

June is the halfway point of the year! The month of June is special for several reasons. Since it is the halfway point of the year, it encourages me to reflect back over the first part of the year at goals accomplished, and adventures and memories made. I also think about the goals, adventures, and memories I still want to accomplish and create. June is also important to me for two other special reasons. One, it marks the end of another school year! As a teacher, this is super exciting news!! Second, it's my birthday month! 2023 was extra special because I entered a new decade. I turned 40 on June 4th!! I can't believe 40 years of life have already gone by! It doesn't seem that long, and I know I don't look it. I love seeing people trying to guess my age. It's true though! In my last decade, I have experienced great adventures, heartache, disappointments, challenges, accomplished goals, new connections, and new memories. Yes, it was filled with moments of struggles and challenges, but it was also filled with moments of growth and excitement. It's been growth that is helping towards my journey to wholeness. I'm thankful I made it and I'm still standing with God! As this book comes to a close, I want to take a moment and reflect on the last decade of my life. Since I love words, I am going to use six words to describe the last decade of my life:

1. <u>Life-changing</u>- As a young woman, I have seen myself change and grow in so many ways. Over the 10 years, I have lost a lot of loved ones that were near and dear to my heart. I miss all of them very much! Both of my parents passed before I reached this new decade. Losing both of your parents is hard and their loss hit me hard. Both were

unexpected. I remember every detail of their last days. Daddy passed on April 14, 2002 from a heart attack. Mom passed away on January 18, 2020 after a brief illness in the hospital. Almost 18 years separated Momma and Daddy's passing. For so long after Daddy passed, it had been my brother, Mom, and me. In the unexpected, I thank God for him continuing to change and grow me. Even when the circumstances changed, God never did! I'm not the same woman I was on that early Sunday morning when Daddy left and that early Saturday morning when Momma left. In fact, I'm not the same woman I was 2 years ago, 2 months ago, even 2 days ago. I am continually evolving and I love that!

2. <u>New beginnings</u>- I got a new look as I'm wearing glasses now! It took me a little while to get used to them, but I love them and how they look classy! In 2019, I started my blogging journey and thankful that continues 4 years later. My blog is Queen Jen's Gems and can be found at https://queenjen129.blogspot.com. In 2020, I became an author by publishing many of my devotionals in my first book titled <u>Grow Gracefully: Devotions To Change You From The Inside Out</u>. At work, I moved from being a teacher assistant to working with Reading students to being a full-time teacher with my own classroom. That all happened in my last decade- God is good! When I wanted to give up, I knew I couldn't because God was calling me to greater and to teach and impact the next generation. In 2021, I received my Master's degree of Elementary Education while working full-time and losing my Mom the year before I got my degree. In turn, that helped me begin my new chapter of teaching full-time. I currently teach 6th grade Language Arts and Reading. In 2023, I received my gifted education endorsement certification online to increase my knowledge even more. I became a blogger, author, and teacher all

within the last decade! I'm so grateful for those new chapters and the new chapters to come.

3. <u>Challenging</u>- As I mentioned earlier, I have loss lots of loved ones with my most recent relative, my great aunt who I had gotten very close to. It's hard losing those close to you. I also experienced hurt and rejection in relationships. Life itself has brought challenging times with circumstances that hurt. When I received my Master's degree and begin my teaching career, it happened in the middle of a pandemic. Whew! Talk about challenging! The teacher tests I had to take were all challenging as I do not like taking tests. I did study, but I didn't pass all of them the 1st time. In fact, some of them I had to take at least 2 or more times to pass. My Math teacher test took 3 times to pass. Finally, I passed that in the summer of 2022! I also feel like I really locked in on my solid friend circle in this last decade. Before that, I knew some that was supposed to be in my friend circle. However, this decade really helped me see who belonged and who I could trust. I can't and don't trust everyone. I also dealt with health issues that came in the form of covid, strep, fibroids, and a blood transfusion, which resulted in me finding out I have anemia. I'm constantly working on getting more sleep and rest, but I am getting more iron rich foods in me and getting regular check-ups.

4. <u>Community</u>- I have the best support system ever! My support system is made up of family, friends, co-workers, and church family members. When going through my challenging circumstances, I can count on my people to come through. In my hurt and loss, they stood by me. In my wins and progress, they celebrate with me. They continue to encourage me. Over this last decade, my community has really embraced me and helped me to embrace who I am. I

have drawn closer to my community and our bond becomes stronger each day.

5. <u>Adventurous</u>- I have had so many fun and new experiences in this last decade. Last year in 2022, my family started having family fun days where we get together and have a good time and may go out to eat, bowl, visit a new place, etc. It can be for a special occasion or not. What matters to us is that we are taking time to be together and make new memories. I have been able to visit state parks, an art show, the mountains, beaches, new restaurants, and new places in general. I attended Sunflower and Daffodil festivals for the first time. I love flowers, which made it even better! Roses are my favorite flower, but sunflowers are starting to creep up and knock out roses for 1st place. I enjoyed weddings and wedding anniversaries, church events, and birthday and graduation celebrations with those nearest and dearest to my heart. I am learning to see every moment and new experience as an adventure. I also received a great gift a week before Christmas in 2023 that will expand those adventures in the future. Guess what the gift is?! It's my passport! I applied in November 2023 as it's a goal I've been wanting to do for a while. I stepped out on faith and it came a few weeks later. I'm so happy and grateful!! I have loved seeing the world around me and look forward to the adventures that are to come.

6. <u>Growing and Glowing</u>- My motto on this journey! Thanks be to God, I have overcome and still overcoming daily in life. I have grown so much spiritually, in my career, in my relationships, as a woman in general. I continue to let my light shine despite the struggles of missing my people and life in general and negativity that comes my way. I continue to hold on to my joy that God gave me because I know it's him that's given me what I need. I have learned to tell my

people I love them and cherish every hug, smile, visit, conversation, and laugh because we never know when it will be our last with someone. All the lessons have taught me so much and really helped me gain the confidence I have today. I speak with so much more confidence than I used to. I know my voice and ideas matter. What once had me holding my head down, I can now stare it in the face because I know who I am and that I'm growing and thriving. I thank God so much! If you have been a part of my journey in the last 10 years or more, I say from the bottom of my heart: thank you!!!! I can't wait to see what these next 10 years hold. I know it will be great! Here's to 40!! Here's to our journey of wholeness!! May God bless you all!!

Acknowledgements

First, I want to thank God for the opportunity to write my second book! I am so very grateful as my faith is very important to me. God has been with me every step of the way and has continued to bless me with opportunities and open doors. I want to give honor to my parents who raised, loved, and supported me in the time they were here with me. I miss them so much! There's not a day that goes by where I don't see their influence and love shine brightly. Next, I want to thank my family, friends, co-workers, church family, and blog readers who continue to encourage and support me. Your prayers, comments, help, encouragement, and advice are appreciated! Lastly, here's to us! May we continue together in this journey towards wholeness! May God continue to bless you all!

Made in United States
Orlando, FL
17 March 2024